Interviewing with College Coaches

A Guide for Aspiring Student-Athletes and their Families

James F. Plappert

DEDICATION

This book is dedicated to my children, Maddi, Ben, Elly and Hannah, for blessing me with a life filled by their smiles, their love, and above all their inspiration.

TABLE OF CONTENTS

1 CHALLENGES

The College Selection Process:

By itself, today's college selection process is often overwhelming to both students and parents; for the student who wants to play intercollegiate sports the level of angst is even greater. To the student-athlete there seems to be:

- an infinite amount of information available,
- a huge number of potential "institutions of higher learning",
- hundreds of opportunities (both academic and athletic), and
- dozens of factors and minute details which must be considered and controlled.

The "college years" require major investments in both time and money; how can you maximize the student's return on this experience? How can the student-athlete find the right chemistry with the school and the coaching staff while maintaining the academic & athletic balance they personally desire?

This book and its sister publication, *So, You Want to be a College Athlete*, should help to facilitate important, life-directing conversations between students and parents. Parents, are you really satisfied to spend tens of thousands or maybe hundreds of thousands of dollars to send your student-athlete to the university whose school colors or mascot they like the most? Is the school from which you graduated and at which you had such great experiences necessarily the best for your son or daughter? Is that local school, or "name" academic school, or prestigious athletic school the best one for them? The answers to all of these questions are, "Of course not ... well, not necessarily ... but maybe." They *might* be the best schools for them, but don't you think it would be worthwhile to look into finding the **right-fit** college or university to fit the needs, wants and desires of your son or daughter? In the end, you want your child to **flourish**, and that is much more likely to happen at a **right-fit** school.

With so much riding on this decision, both the student-athlete and the family can feel overwhelmed by the power and responsibility of its outcome. It is, perhaps, thus far the biggest, most important decision made by this young adult in his or her life. The decision is "tough" but, in the end, every student-athlete himself or herself needs to "own" their part in this decision.

Adding even more pressure, many coaches start seriously looking at athletes during the athlete's freshman season in high school ... so it's never too early for the student-athlete to begin thinking about the selection process, to begin setting goals, and to begin investigating summer camps at colleges of interest. It's never too early to get on the coach's radar. By fall of their sophomore year the student-athlete should be actively corresponding with **right-fit** college coaches (albeit a "one-way" correspondence, at times, due to NCAA contact rules) and developing their student-athlete resume. Finally, by junior year they should be actively involved in the final selection process because by the end of their junior year, or at the latest, the summer between junior and senior year, in many cases and in many sports in NCAA Divisions I and II, it's all over ... seriously, done deal. The bottom line: the time to act is **now**.

The Recruiting Process:

To successfully compete in this arena, the student-athlete must:

- Be totally aware of and follow all applicable NCAA recruiting guidelines,
- Fully understand the do's and don'ts and the inner workings of the college athletics recruiting process,
- Fully understand their own wants, desires, and needs when it comes to finding that ***right-fit*** institution for them,
- Have a well-developed, informative, student-athlete resume,
- Have a well-prepared video available on DVD or YouTube,
- Have a well-developed contact and marketing plan, and
- Be well-prepared to meet with, respond to, and interface with the recruiting coaches.

"Some people dream of success ...

while others wake up and work hard at it."

Interviewing with College Coaches:

This particular book is designed to help both the student-athlete and parents with that final step – the face-to-face (or telephone) meeting with the coaches. Its purpose is to provide preparation and guidance in areas that are very foreign to inexperienced high school student interviewers. It answers questions such as:

- What is the objective of an interview?
- What is the process itself, what are the steps?
- What questions will the coach ask?
- What questions should I ask?
- How do I conclude an interview?
- What happens next?
- What if it's over the phone?
- It didn't go well – why?
- I didn't like *them*; now what?

Every student-athlete is different in their academic abilities, in their athletic abilities, and in their personality. The trick is to learn the basics, understand the process, and then fine tune your own actions to fit your own "style."

In the world of business recruiting, the candidates interviewing for an executive level position at a potential employer want to "close the deal." Athletic recruiting is no different. The student-athlete wants to win, to be the one selected, to be "recruited." This guide is written to help him or her "to be the one," to help them ***earn*** their dreams, and to find that ***right-fit*** school for them.

2 OBJECTIVE OF THE INTERVIEW

The first person you'll normally meet on the team's athletic staff will be a head coach or perhaps one of the assistant or position coaches who is in charge of recruiting in your area of the country. While he or she will examine your athletic and academic background as their primary criterion, other important factors under consideration will be your personal strengths & weaknesses, your accomplishments outside of the classroom and off the field, your personality, and how you actually handle yourself during the interview. He or she is also interested in evaluating your level of motivation, your values, and your overall attitude. They need to find out if you are the right person for the position, the team, and the college.

While it's true that an interview is an important screening tool for colleges and coaches, it also allows *you* to learn the things *you* need to know about the coach, the team, and the college so that you can make an intelligent decision about whether they'll fit with *your* plans or not. It pays huge dividends to approach an interview focused on two objectives: gathering information to answer your questions and getting an offer to attend that school and play on that team. Remember, you can't say either "yes" or "no" to them if they don't want you first.

As with almost all situations in life, **preparation is the key to success**; as a top athlete you know that by now. There are no shortcuts. The market for student-athletes is very competitive and you will not be the only qualified player in contention for a position. The deciding factor may simply be the way you present your skills and qualifications relevant to the position you play and how well you present yourself during the interview.

This guide will help you prepare for the interview – to win. Take your time to thoroughly review the material in this book. The tips and techniques outlined have been tested, and they work! They will improve, though not guarantee, your chances of being recruited – your athletic ability and academic ability will ultimately dictate whether you are recruited or not. However, finely honed interviewing skills can give you a definite leg up on other, equally-qualified athletes, if you do the job right. Do your homework. Just like studying for a huge chemistry exam or practicing for the league championship game, **preparing** for meeting the coaches and their assistants is the only way to win. **Do not, to any degree, "wing it."**

3 INTERVIEW OVERVIEW

A. PROPER PREPARATION

Know Yourself – *formally write down answers to these questions:*
(Use the first worksheet in the Appendix, if you'd like)

- What are your strengths? What are your weaknesses? Both academically and athletically.
- What are your short and long term goals? Athletically, academically, in life in general.
- Evaluate yourself in terms of this college and this team. Where do you fit in, what are the plusses and the minuses of playing there? Will you sit on the bench for two years before playing, or will you be an impact player from day one – *does it matter to you?*
- Formulate responses to potential questions by asking yourself the question: "Why should they recruit me?" Conversely, ask yourself the question: "What are the things I like best about this school and why do I want to go there?"

- Remember that you're going to the interview to gather information about the coach, the team, and the college, to sell yourself, and to become a recruited student-athlete.

Research the College, the Team, and the Coach

(Use the second worksheet in the Appendix, if you'd like)

- You'll find almost everything you need on the school's academic and athletic web sites and on the NCAA.com web site to do research and to review details about:
  - ✓ The college – where located, what size town, driving distance from your home, undergraduate population, academic ranking, academic majors, public vs. private, religious affiliation, NCAA Division (I, II, III, or non-member), team ranking in this sport (RPI), conference they play in, amount of travel the team does during their season (some teams miss significantly more classes than others).
  - ✓ The team – class ratios (number of freshmen, sophomores, juniors, and seniors – do freshmen tend to stay on the team through their senior year?), win-loss records, opponents, leading players, captains, etc.
  - ✓ The coaches – where did they play, backgrounds, styles, career win-loss records, etc.
  - ✓ Now, do all (or most) of the answers fit with your criteria for the type of school you'd like to attend?
- The Internet also offers a wealth of *additional* information (look at the college's and team's press releases on their web site, the school paper, and the closest major newspaper's articles about the school, the team, the coach, and the competitors they've played).
- Talk to your high school counselors and athletic staff (coaches and administrators) to see what they know about the school, its coaches, and its athletic and academic reputation.
- Talk to your club coach or director to gather any information they may be able to offer.
- Be prepared to tell the interviewer why their school and their team are attractive to you.

B. WHAT TO BRING & WHEN TO ARRIVE

Items to Bring to the Interview:

- Student-Athlete Resume:
  - ✓ Review your resume thoroughly and be prepared to discuss all points listed in it, both academic and athletic.
  - ✓ Always bring two hard copies of your resume identical to the one supplied to the interviewer via email.
- Your current sport-appropriate statistics – hard copy.
- Your SAT or ACT scores and high school transcripts (note: not having scores or grades may imply that they are "low;" these unofficial scores and transcripts are used for admissions "reads").
- Notepad and pen to jot down notes. Your own questions for the coaches should be pre-written into this notebook.
- Prepare and review your questions (see Chapters 3 and 4) as well as specific responses.
- Directions to the interview location as well as the interviewer's phone number in case you are running late (**but don't be … ever**).
- *Do not take cell phones into an interview (unless they are turned OFF) – this also applies to all accompanying family members.*

Arrival at the Interview:

- Arrive **no earlier** than fifteen minutes before the set interview time, but **no later** than five minutes prior to the interview time.
- Allow adequate time for traffic, parking, and a last-minute appearance check. If possible, scout out the location earlier in the day or even the day before in order to avoid any last minute problems.
- Review your notes and go in with **confidence** (because you *are* prepared!).

C. YOUR APPEARANCE

- Wear appropriate clothing – business casual (not sloppy, not dressy); remember, you will be representing your college and your team when travelling to away games – appearance counts, so try to look as you would when travelling with the team. Men, if the team travels in suits or sports coats, wear that. You can never undo a *first* impression.

- Avoid exotic hairstyles and excessive makeup. Hair should be neat, clean and brushed. Women, makeup should be light and natural looking.
- Use deodorant but avoid heavy colognes or fragrances.
- Jewelry should be limited and subtle.
- **Maintain good eye contact.**

D. THE INTERVIEW

- Interviews at the school are generally with the head coach first, then an interview with the assistant or position coach, or vice-versa, or a joint interview with both coaches simultaneously. Be flexible, as any variation may be the norm with this coaching staff.
- Be honest and be consistent. All interviewers *will* compare their thoughts after the interview. People who misspeak are often said to be "caught in a lie," but have you ever heard of someone being "caught in the truth?"
- **Note:** For all interviews:
  - ✓ Shake hands firmly, maintaining good eye contact with the interviewer during the handshake.
  - ✓ Maintain a high energy level.
  - ✓ Sit up with your back straight.
  - ✓ Maintain good eye contact throughout the interview – yes, this is the third time this has been mentioned on this page alone – it's *very important*.
  - ✓ It is to your advantage if a subject of mutual interest arises, but do not fake knowledge.
  - ✓ Be yourself; remember you are looking for a ***right-fit*** situation.
  - ✓ Poise, confidence, and self-respect are of great importance.

✓ Be an "active listener." Only by listening carefully will you know what the coach is really looking for. **Remember, you have two ears and only one mouth – use them in that ratio.**

• If you need financial aid, make sure to ask questions about this school's financial aid programs to further clarify what you've already learned while doing your research prior to the interview; don't worry, they'll get very specific about your personal financial aid later in the recruiting process.

The coaches will usually provide both college and team information and facts, but will also ask questions (see Chapter 3) about you, your skills, and your teams' successes. As you answer, remember that the interviewers are trying to see how you can contribute to their team.

Conduct yourself with confidence and determination to get recruited. If you are prepared, there is no reason to be nervous. You will have options at other schools, of course, and your interviewer knows this, but wants to think that you want to play with *this* team. Don't play coy; again, be honest if asked about these teams and schools.

Sell yourself. This is your first (and, at times, only) face-to-face meeting and the opportunity to play here may well depend on your presentation. You must present a positive attitude to the coaches. You must *never* seem disinterested or appear to be just shopping around for the highest scholarship; that's always a turn-off. Go ahead, let your honest enthusiasm and informed curiosity show.

The interview should be a two-way conversation. Ask questions of the coaches. This shows your interest in both the school and the team. It also enables you to gather the right information to make an intelligent decision *for you* afterwards. The questions you have prepared can be asked to the different people who interview you.

You may ask questions that will confirm or further clarify information that you have already researched. For example:

- If there are 8 new recruits on the team every year and this year there are only 2 juniors on the roster, ask what happened that the others are not on the roster?
- Freshman playing time can be gleaned from last year's cumulative stats shown on the web; why are some players getting triple (or more) playing time over some of their classmates and others getting no time at all on the field?

In some cases the coach will openly discuss these types of questions, in others it's really not public information (the player left school, had medical issues, experienced psychological issues, etc.). Those types of cases would simply be "normal attrition."

This type of questioning will help you to better understand the coach, the coach's needs, and the team's profile.

Remember that your objectives in the interview are to gather information and to be recruited. During the interview you must gather enough information concerning the college, the team, and the coach to make a decision as to whether this is the *right-fit* for you.

The college recruiting interview is like looking to buy a new house; at times you may have to travel out of town to see them. Therefore, you want to gather as much information as possible while you are there since ultimately you may be paying a high price for what you want.

E. ADVICE FOR PARENTS

- Work with your child prior to the interview to help them to be fully prepared for this very important event.
- If you are invited to attend the interview with your student-athlete, please remember that this is his or her interview with the staff, not your interview – please, stay in the background. As it pertains to the interview itself, the parents' have **one** important job – to drive the car so your student-athlete is in attendance – no more, no less.
- The coach wants to see how your child handles himself or herself, how they might behave when you're not there. They want to see and hear what your son or daughter has to say and how they say it.

- On the other hand, they will see how you interact with each other as a family unit and will be noting that, too – mutual respect and confidence in each other is always a good thing.
- To that end, do not answer questions for your son or daughter
  - ✓ Do not provide stats, win-loss records, or anything else you might personally know (many parents tend to know this stuff) **unless** your son or daughter specifically asks for your help – which is perfectly all right.
  - ✓ Do not answer any question unless it is directed specifically to you; at all other times be quiet and respectful of the situation.
  - ✓ Be like a fan in the stands at your student-athlete's games: positive and supportive.
- A major point here – the coaches are looking at you, too. If everything goes well, *your* family will be a major part of *their* family for the next four years or so – and this is one instance where the coach gets to pick his or her future "relatives." Be on your best and friendliest behavior.
- Do not act like your son's or daughter's agent trying to "cut a deal." This is a real turn-off to most coaches.
  - ✓ That being said, in many cases this interview is the only interview your student-athlete will have with this school and the coaches are happy to discuss financial aid and scholarships with you. Now that they are no longer permitted by the NCAA to *email* a recruit about scholarships (athletic or academic) they almost have to discuss this with the student-athlete when he or she comes onto campus or if the recruit telephones them (within NCAA guidelines, of course).
- ***Do not take cell phones into an interview (unless they are turned OFF).***

4 TYPICAL INTERVIEWER'S QUESTIONS & RESPONSES

You should give complete but brief and *relaxed* answers to questions. When possible use the coach's questions as a basis for developing information that you want to make sure is covered. Continue to sell yourself in an honest, positive way.

When answering questions, include short stories involving academic and/or athletic (as appropriate) problems or challenges you faced and how you were able to resolve them. Describe the results you achieved. **Do not make these stories up** (it's just too evident when that occurs), but rather use concrete examples that have happened to you in the classroom, on the field, or in your day-to-day life.

Be strong enough to answer the tough questions that you will be asked by being **prepared** for them – just like you are for the big game.

A. Exploring your Background Questions

Tell me about yourself.

Answer these questions in terms of the qualifications required for the position being played. Keep responses concise and brief. Avoid being derogatory or negative about coaches, opponents, officials, teammates, or just about anything – be positive.

"Tell me about yourself" really means, "Tell me about your qualifications to play on this team and to attend this college." You should prepare a one-to-two minute discussion (no more) before the interview addressing those issues. Practice your responses with a parent or teammate. Do they agree with your self-analysis?

What are your greatest strengths?

Coaches like to hear abstract qualities as well as academic and athletic prowess. Loyalty, willingness to work hard, eagerness, fast-learner, good sport-appropriate skills, politeness, and promptness, all expressed in concrete terms are good examples.

What are your greatest weaknesses?

Do not be intimidated by this question; we all have weaknesses. How you respond to the question itself is what the coach is most likely listening for, not necessarily your exact weaknesses. The coach probably wants either (a) reassurance that bringing you onboard won't be a mistake and/or (b) to see if you are aware of your own weaknesses and what you might be doing to improve. This is **not** the time to confess all your life's imperfections. (Do not state "not being able to go to goal as often as I'd like", or "doing all the runs in practice", etc.). **Present your weaknesses as problems that you have solved or will be solving.** Do not be smug about your answer and, as always, be honest. A story about a weakness that you have corrected or overcome is often a good example. A couple of examples might be something like, "I struggled during the off season with back spasms, so I'm attending core strengthening sessions twice a week at my local health club" or "I've always had a problem with standardized tests, so I'm currently in the middle of a 6-week SAT prep course." Don't talk about corrective actions you *might* take, instead talk about what you *are* doing or have done. Be proactive. Start now.

B. Personality Questions

What do you do in your spare time?

Sports, sports, sports *only* does not necessarily make Jack or Jill a top recruit. Present yourself as a well-rounded person. Your answer should give you dimension. Name some hobbies, some academic pursuits, some community or religious-related activities, tutoring your niece or nephew, anything that helps the interviewer to understand who you are as a person. This is also a good place to talk about that summer or part-time job.

C. Motivation & Drive Questions

Answer "what motivates and drives you" questions enthusiastically. Show the coach that you are interested in this college and that you really want to be on this team. Remember to maintain eye contact and be sincere. If you've done your research, you'll have no problem here.

How can you contribute to this team?

Be positive and sell your skills. Strong athletic skills, enthusiasm, and the desire to compete and win are good responses.

Why should I recruit you for this team?

Explain your athletic and academic qualifications and how they fit the college and the team. Address your interest in the team, the coach, and the college and why you would enjoy playing there. Emphasize your ability to successfully contribute to the team.

Why do you want to come to our school?

Compliment the college, its location, or its faculty. Other positive remarks might be about the college's range of majors or some particular work a professor has done (remember your research? – use it now).

What interests you most about this team?

Teasing the interviewer with a truthful one or two-word answer such as, "the challenge" or "the opportunity," will force them to ask you to explain. Here again, you have the chance to demonstrate your knowledge of the team and its players and what you might be able to contribute.

What are your career goals?

"I don't know" is *not* an acceptable answer. No one is going to deny you the flexibility to change your plans; they just want to be sure you *have* goals and plans that can be addressed at this school. If you want to be a physical therapist and this school does not offer that major, well, there is a definite disconnect between what you want and what they offer.

Your answer should depend on a specific time frame:

Short term – something like, "During my four years here, I want to be the best I can be on the field and in the classroom. To contribute to the team in any way possible and to prepare myself for the future"

Long term – One answer might be, "After graduating, I see myself … [your answer]." However, many students, like their declared major, are "undecided." If you really don't know what you want to do in the long haul, give broad-brushed ideas about what you are interested in academically or professionally.

What are you doing to achieve your goals?

Think about this answer and fine tune it for your own situation and goals: "I want to be a high school teacher, so in the summers I've been working as a camp counselor to get the feel for working with kids," or "Since I'd like to be a hotel administration major, I've worked in a theme park for the last two summers." Also, what do you do to achieve your athletic goals?

Are you looking at any other colleges?

Share your short list of schools in which you are genuinely interested. Your list paints a clear picture of what kind of school you'd like to attend.

In your answer, show that your college search is geared toward similar institutions and/or teams. This demonstrates a well-defined, focused objective (as, hopefully, it really is). Make it known that you are exploring ways to maximize your potential and are serious about finding the perfect *right-fit* opportunity.

It is always good to tell the coach that their school is "right at the top of my list" – if it weren't, why would you be there? Don't give any indication that you are just shopping, as hopefully you are not. By the time you sit down in front of the coach for an interview, you should have thoroughly investigated your own wants and needs for college and have decided that this school is a good fit for those criteria. Use the worksheets in the Appendix to help you through this thought process.

One Division I coach summarized answers to this question as follows: "When we hear 'top five' we read that as 'You are number five on my list.' We prefer to hear that we are in a group of five schools that feel like a good fit, ideally in the top one, two, or three. Any more than that, in list form, and we don't stand a chance."

If this school is your absolute top pick, the one you've dreamed of attending since you were in grade school – tell them – then work together to make it happen!

The bottom line is that coaches are looking for players who want to play at *their* school on *their* team with *their* players!

In preparing for these questions remember that, in addition to all of the research that you've done on your own, you have other resources to tap if needed: your parents, your friends, your teammates, your high school counselors, athletic director, and teachers, and your high school and club coaches. You'd be wise to use any or all of these resources to talk with and/or to practice your interviewing skills with as you wind your way on your journey to finding the **right-fit** college for you.

5 QUESTIONS FOR *YOU* TO ASK

Interviews should be two-way conversations. You must ask questions and take an active role in the interview. Asking questions gives you a chance to demonstrate your depth of knowledge about the college, the team, and the coach as well as to establish an easy flow of conversation and a relaxed atmosphere between you and the coaches. Building this kind of rapport is always a plus in an interview.

An important note here: coaches are generally impressed by written, pre-prepared questions because the very act of pre-thinking and writing down these questions demonstrates just how well you prepare yourself for important situations, both on and off of the field.

Remember, you are not just there for the interviewer to determine if you are right for the team, but your questions can help you determine if this college and team and coach are right for you. Many of your questions should evolve from the research you've done to prepare for the interview.

Here are some general guidelines for your questions.

- Don't *cross-examine* the coach. Questions should be part of the flow of the interview; nothing accusatory or blatantly negative should be on your list. If the team went 2-14 last season, a good way to address this issue might be, "I see that last year's record was nothing like it has been in the past. What's the strategy for next season to let you get back to your winning ways?"

- Ask questions requiring an explanation. Questions that can be answered with a simple "yes" or "no" are *conversation stoppers* and should be avoided. The questions you ask should add to your breadth of knowledge about the school. Examples:
  - ✓ Conversation stopper: "Is there an off-season conditioning program?"
  - ✓ Good question: "What are the requirements of your off season strength and conditioning program?"

- Don't ever interrupt when the coach is answering a question that *you* asked.

- Ask relevant questions. Focus on the college, the coach, the team, and the situation.

- Select about 10-12 questions from the following lists that are particularly interesting to you. Write them down in the notebook that you will take with you to the interview so you can pull it out (to show how prepared you are) when the coach asks, "Do you have any questions for me?" You do not have to ask them all, just whatever feels comfortable and fits the situation at hand.

- It is entirely appropriate to take notes as the coach answers.

Note to Coaches: If you're reading this book, you might want to do your research and have answers to these questions pre-prepared (yes, you should be doing your research and preparing, too).

POTENTIAL QUESTIONS:

A. About the Team

1. How many players do you typically carry on your roster?
2. How many players will you be looking to recruit in my graduating class of 20XX and for what specific positions?
3. Do you play freshmen on a regular basis? Under what criteria?
4. Does the entire squad travel to away games or only select players? What are the criteria for selecting those players?
5. How much travel does the team do during the season? Are there college or conference/league restrictions on travel?
6. Are there differences in the roles of scholarship vs. non-scholarship athletes? What are they? How many players of each type are currently on your roster?
7. Do you hold try outs? If so, how are they run?
8. Describe the personality of the team. Do I fit?
9. How many players can you "support" each year in the admissions process? How does this work?

B. About the Program

1. Describe a typical week for your players during season. What is the normal regimen during off season?
2. What summer activities do the players normally participate in?
3. What are the program's goals for both next season and for the longer term?
4. Are you satisfied that the program receives good budgetary support from the administration? What could they do better?
5. Do the students at the school generally support the team? What's the average attendance for home games?
6. Tell me about the facilities – anything new in the near future?
7. What equipment does each player receive? Do I need to supply anything for myself?

8. When are practices held during the season – mornings, afternoons, evenings? What hours? What about practices during off season?

9. What does the strength and conditioning program require?

10. Are incoming freshman normally (or ever) red-shirted? Under what circumstances?

11. Does the team typically use all the permissible training hours in season, off season and during nontraditional season? What about any training in addition to sport specific training – lifting, conditioning, sports psychology, etc.?

C. About the Coach

1. What is your personal coaching philosophy and style?

2. Describe your normal, day-to-day interactions with your individual players during the season.

3. Describe your communication style.

4. How long have you been at this school (note: you should know the answer to this … remember your research?) and how long do you plan on staying?

5. Tell me about a typical practice – what role do you play and what role do your assistants play?

D. About Academics

1. Will I miss many classes because of games and travel? Does the faculty generally support the athletic community? Are any special provisions made for athletes?

2. What percentage of the team's players graduate in four years (or "on time")? What is the graduation rate? What is the normal attrition rate?

3. What are typical majors for the team's athletes?

4. Does this school use the Athletic Index (AI) for admissions and team recruiting purposes? What are the guidelines for your recruiting efforts, specifically?

5. What SAT's and GPA's are required to be a recruited athlete?

6. What is the team's GPA and how does it compare to the student body at large?
7. What academic support is available for athletes?
8. Tell me what happens when there are conflicts between practices and classes.
9. Is priority scheduling available for athletes? How does it work?

E. About Campus Life

1. Do your freshman players live together? If not, what are typical housing arrangements? What about the upper class years – what typically happens then?
2. Do you require your athletes to live on campus? What is the availability of on-campus housing?
3. Do your athletes participate in Greek life or other social clubs or activities?
4. Are your student-athletes able to have a job? Doing what?
5. What is your personal philosophy on a team member studying abroad?
6. (If appropriate) How do you handle student teaching semesters for education majors?

F. About Financial Aid

1. Coach, what can you tell me about financial aid?
2. What is the availability of athletic scholarships at this college? How many can you offer? What about other forms of financial aid? Academic scholar-ships? Need-based scholarships? Can they all be combined?
3. Have you ever decreased an athletic scholarship? Why?
4. Have you ever not renewed an athletic scholarship? Why?
5. Do you ever increase scholarships? Why?
6. If a player is injured and no longer able to play, would you re-new their scholarship?
7. (For "need based" financial aid institutions … again, do your research) How would you describe your financial aid packages?

G. About Your Status as a Recruit

1. Among your current recruits, where do I rank athletically? What tier am I in? How many are in your first tier?

2. You now know my academic abilities, where do I rank there? Will my SAT's and GPA qualify me for this school and my proposed major?

3. What do I need to do athletically or academically to be your top recruit for this year?

4. Am I one of the athletes you will recommend to admissions? How does that work?

5. Do you need anything else from me to aid in your decision-making process?

6 CONCLUDING THE INTERVIEW

FOR THE *BLUE CHIP*, HIGHLY RECRUITED ATHLETE:

The concluding questions would likely be coming from the coach, something like, "What is your decision making timeline," and, "Are we in your top two?" These athletes need to be prepared to answer those questions. In many cases the first interview occurs at the same time as an invited unofficial overnight visit. Coaches don't typically offer those to a player they aren't seriously considering. If you're in this classification, **be prepared** to honestly answer the types of questions above.

ALL OTHERS, IF YOU ARE INTERESTED:

If you are **sincerely interested** in the team and the college and are satisfied with the answers given so far during the interview, you should ask the coach if he/she feels you are the right person for their team. This gives you another chance to review points that may need clarification. Illustrate confidence in your abilities and convince the coach that you are capable of playing successfully on this team and succeeding academically at this school.

Ask to be one of their recruits. Make a positive statement about the team, the coach, or the college. Emphasize that this is exactly the type of situation you've been looking for and that you would like to be offered a spot on the team. Ask what the next step might be. A typical conclusion might be:

> "Thank you for this meeting, Coach Smith. I like what I've heard today and I'd love to join your team. I know I'd be an asset to you and your team because you need someone who can [state their need] and who is [state a needed quality]. I think I could fill that role because I [state how you fill the need or have that quality].
>
> "As you know, I have [match your qualifications with the coach's needs].
>
> "Before I leave, do you have any more questions about my background or accomplishments or can I supply you with any more information?
>
> "On a scale of 1 to 10, how do I compare to the other recruits you've interviewed? Where do I rank on your list of potential recruits?
>
> "Ok, what happens next?"

The farewell should also include a smile, **direct eye contact**, and a firm handshake.

IF YOU ARE DISINTERESTED OR HESITANT:

If you are **sincerely not interested** in either the team or the college based on what you've heard during the interview or are not satisfied with some of the answers given, you should express your hesitation to the coach. Remember, always be honest, but phrase your hesitation in terms that will lead to a confirmation of your hesitation or a positive resolution of the feeling. The reason for your hesitation may be based on an honest misunderstanding of the facts or the situation at hand and you certainly do not want to "burn any bridges" (see Chapter 10). A typical conclusion might be:

> "Thank you for this meeting, Coach Smith. I'm somewhat concerned about one aspect of what I've heard today and I'd love to discuss it with you. I think I understand that [state the problem]. Is that correct, and, if so, what are you planning to do about it?"

If the situation is resolved by the answer to that question, then proceed as above for a "sincere interest" closing.

If the situation is not resolved by the answer to your concluding question, state something like the following:

> "Thank you for your honest answer. Before I leave, do you have any more questions about my background or accomplishments or can I supply you with any more information?"

The farewell should then include a smile, **direct eye contact**, and a firm handshake.

Think about why you are **hesitant** on your way home and talk about it with your parents, your high school coach or AD, your school's guidance counselor, or maybe a trusted teammate. If it's at all resolvable, send a positive follow-up note to the coach (see Chapter 6), if it's definitely not resolvable, cut the process short and move on to your next college choices. Make sure you send a follow-up note (or a phone call) to the coach advising him or her of your decision.

Remember that it is entirely normal to be hesitant. It's just human nature. If you are hesitant about this opportunity, if you're just not sure, or if you have mixed feelings, be sure to figure out exactly why you feel this way. You may have to readjust your college selection criteria based on these feelings if your other college choices have similar characteristics. Adjusting now can save lots of heartache later.

Did you love the campus and the tour guide but not really like the coach? Did you like the coach and campus but didn't really care for several of the players you met or the team profile they represent? Did you like the coach, but got some bad vibes about him or her from some of the players? Was everything just great about the coach and the team, but this is an urban school and you were really looking for something a little more in the country? Do you want to major in Physical Therapy … or Nursing … or Russian Literature … or Education … and they simply don't offer that option?

Whatever the reason, you'll want to resolve these feelings by looking over and reviewing your own worksheets (see Appendix) to see if you can really get what you want from this school and its academic and athletic programs. Again, talk about it with your parents, your high school coach, your counselor, and maybe a trusted teammate.

Until such feelings are resolved one way or the other, stay in touch with the coach on a positive basis and keep looking for the answers that will resolve your dilemma.

If the school is seriously interested in you, you should hold off on a decision until after you have an overnight visit. On this visit, you will be spending much more time with potential teammates and in classes than you will with the coaches. An overnight visit isn't foolproof but it provides you with the opportunity to interact with players while not under the eye of the coaching staff. You can gather fantastic amounts of data about the school, the team, and the coaches to assist you in your decision-making.

7 FOLLOW-UP EMAIL

It is always necessary to send a short note of appreciation to thank the coach and the other interviewers for their time, effort, and consideration shown when meeting with you.

See the following two pages for examples of emails to send when you are either interested or sincerely disinterested in the college, team, or coach after your interview.

IF YOU ARE INTERESTED:

Reiterate your interest in the team and the college as well as your ability to contribute. Be sure to email your correspondence the following day. This is a good way to keep your name current in the coach's mind. Following is a sample thank-you email that you can adapt to fit your specifics. Personalize this as appropriate.

Monday, January 3, 2012

Dear Coach Smith,

    I want to thank you for the great meeting we had on Saturday, January 1. I am very impressed with both you and Coach Jones, the plans you have for the team, and the academic and athletic facilities at ABC University. Thanks, also, for the informative campus tour. I am very interested in attending ABC and playing [name sport] for you.

    If you have any additional questions about me or my abilities, please don't hesitate to contact me directly or contact my high school coach, Pat Brown at pbrown@school.org or (215) 555-1212.

    Thank you again for the opportunity to meet you.

Sincerely,
Chris Davis
Class of 20XX
cdavis25@gmail.com
(215) 555-2121

Don't forget to send the thank-you email; it's a very important step in showing your continued interest.

IF YOU ARE SINCERELY DISINTERESTED:

If you **firmly establish** that this is not the school or team or coach for you, you must let them know of your choice. Be sure to email (or, even better, phone) the coach as soon as this decision is final (but **do not** take this step until you are certain). Following is a sample thank-you email that you can adapt to fit your specifics. Again, personalize as appropriate.

Monday, January 3, 2012

Dear Coach Smith,

Thank you for the meeting we had on Saturday, January 1. I was very impressed with both you and Coach Jones and the academic and athletic facilities at ABC University. Thanks, also, for the informative and interesting campus tour.

Regrettably, after doing all of my homework on ABC University, I find that it is not the right school for me. I am looking for [say why the fit's not there]. ABC just doesn't fit my needs.

Thank you again for the opportunity to meet with you and Coach Jones.

Sincerely,
Chris Davis,
Class of 20XX
cdavis25@gmail.com
(215) 555-2121

Send the follow-up note or make the phone call; it's the right thing to do.

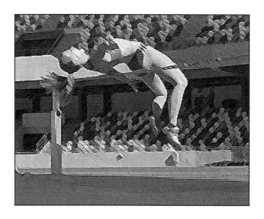

8 TELEPHONE INTERVIEWS

Many coaches conduct telephone interviews (when properly allowed by NCAA rules) to screen student-athletes for basic qualifications, personality, and rapport. It is also an alternative when it is not practical for an out-of-area player to come to the campus.

Many coaches use the phone interview to develop a pool of players to look at more closely and to pare down the number of candidates. The advantages of the phone interview to the coach are that the cost is less, the questions can be standardized, and it can be done quickly.

The aims on both sides of the telephone are limited. The coach (or assistant or position coach) wants a selection of qualified players, and the process screens out many candidates. If the call is a straightforward screening call, the caller will likely ask about your athletic experience, interest in their school, and your academic credentials. Your strategy is to provide facts that support your resume, with some context about your abilities. To be most effective, try using numbers and facts; however, you don't want to volunteer anything that could disqualify you at this juncture. Make every effort to sound professional and personable, as appropriate.

Telephone interviews can be challenging because it is more difficult to gain rapport with the interviewer simply because you cannot see the interviewer's non-verbal reactions and cues. Conversely, the interviewer cannot see your enthusiastic expressions or athletic appearance. This places more weight on your phone manners, clarity of speech, and voice tone as well as on the content of your answers.

5 tips for successfully handling telephone interviews:

1. **Be prepared for the call:**
   - ✓ Be on time and don't get wrapped up in other activities when you're expecting the interviewer to call.
   - ✓ Turn call-waiting off so your call isn't interrupted.
   - ✓ Select a quiet, private room with a telephone in good working condition and its battery fully charged. Turn off the music and TV; close the door.
   - ✓ Arrange the following items: a notepad and pen, your calendar (for Junior Day invitations or other campus visits), your resume, highlights of your own research and brief talking points. If possible, have the team website already pulled up on your computer or phone. That way if something comes up in the conversation you look right on top of things.
   - ✓ Keep a glass of water handy to whet your whistle.
2. **Be prepared for the interview:**
   - ✓ Treat this interview just as you would a face-to-face interview.
   - ✓ Conduct a mock telephone interview with a parent, coach, teammate, counselor, or friend to gain feedback on your voice quality and speech.
   - ✓ Prepare for the phone interview just like you would a face-to-face meeting (see everything above in this guide … especially the sections on research).
   - ✓ Take notes when appropriate.

✓ During the interview, if the interviewer inadvertently answers a question from your prepared list, cross it off. If you don't and forget that it was covered and then ask it yourself, it will seem as if you were not listening.

✓ Use this highly effective question-answering technique for difficult questions: repeat or re-phrase the question then state your answer. This tells the caller that you listened carefully, that you understand the question, and gives you a bit of time to think about your answer.

✓ Avoid simple "yes/no" answers to questions; add your personal selling points at every opportunity. Selling points are nothing more than strengths and other plusses that you would bring to the team. Use the answers you've developed in the "Strengths" category of the *Know Yourself Worksheet* in the Appendix. Write these down and keep them handy during your call.

3. **Present yourself professionally:**

✓ Breathe deeply and relax.

✓ Speak slowly, clearly and with purpose.

✓ Smile, it has a positive effect on your speech patterns which the person on the other end can sense – besides, this is fun.

✓ Don't chew gum, eat or drink anything. It all telegraphs to your listener – right into their ear.

✓ Standing up makes your voice sound stronger.

✓ Be enthusiastic. The first 15 seconds of the call are crucial and an enthusiastic tone in your voice is key. Simply the way you answer the phone has an impact on the caller. Talk distinctly and with confidence.

4. **Follow proper telephone etiquette:**

✓ Be courteous and try not to speak over the interviewer. If you do, apologize and let the interviewer continue.

✓ If you think of a question or comment while the interviewer is speaking, jot a note on your "talking points" list so you will remember it later; don't interrupt them right then.

✓ If you need time to think, say so – as on the radio, silence during a telephone conversation is "dead air time" and should be avoided, if possible.

5. **End the call smoothly:**

✓ Before ending the call, be sure you know the next step in the process, and offer to provide any additional information.

✓ At the end of the call, give up control. The end of the call is always a tricky thing. A good suggestion is to thank the caller for his or her time and say that you are very interested in this team and college. If the interviewer has not told you, it is a good idea to ask, "Coach, what is the next step in the recruiting process?" Let the interviewer re-establish control of the interview with this question.

✓ Do not hang up until the interviewer has hung up.

✓ **Promptly send a formal follow-up email, just as you would for a face-to-face interview.**

9 TOP TEN REASONS FOR REJECTION – PLUS ONE

"I was rejected by the coach … but why?"

There can be many reasons for rejection from an intercollegiate athletic team. The two most important *may* be beyond your control:

1. **Not enough athletic ability** for what the coach needs, or

2. **Not enough academic talent** for what the school needs.

At this point, **ask** the coach why you're not on the top of their list. Is it athletic, academic, or both? This is inherently a tough question to ask, but if you don't ask the question, you'll just be guessing at the answer. Guessing or assuming is always a bad choice when simply asking the question may give you much better insight into the problem and possible paths you may take to resolve this impasse. You didn't get this far by being timid; it's time to stand up and fight.

If you've started the recruiting and selection process early enough in your high school career, you can make a sincere attempt to correct either of these problems, if needed. Ask specifically what it is you need to work on and, if you could correct it, would the coach reassess you in the future as a student-athlete? If so, **act** to correct the problem.

Athletically you can join a club team for more touches or more experience, join a fitness center to work on strength or quickness conditioning, get special coaching – whatever the deficiency is, take steps to solve it and revisit with the coach at a later time.

Academically, if you're close to the target range, retake the SAT's or ACT's, get special tutoring, work with your teachers – again, whatever the deficiency is, take steps to solve it and revisit with the coach at a later time.

In all honesty, if you're toward the end of your high school career and couldn't possibly act to overcome either of these objections, put this school behind you and move on to a more appropriate (for you) *right-fit* institution. Or, if you have sufficient academic credentials and still want to attend this school you may have several athletic options: apply to this school and get in – then either try out to be on the varsity team or be a "walk-on" (ask the coach if they're included on the team) or you can elect to play either a club sport or intramurals. There **can be** options – good ones.

3. Poor attitude: Some star recruits come across as arrogant. While *proven* players can afford to be somewhat self-centered, new recruits cannot … ever. Confidence in your athletic ability is good and confidence in your academic ability is good, but some humility is also *always* good. Oh, and learn to laugh *at* yourself; it's never a bad thing.

4. Inappropriate Appearance or Presence: Some players do not consider their appearance as much as they should. "First impressions" are made in the first three or so minutes of a face-to-face interview. Review the appearance checklist – again, you will be representing the team, the college, and the coaching staff while on the road. Show the coach you can make them proud.

Additionally, the way you present yourself (your "presence," your mode of conduct, your behavior, or your comportment) needs to be appropriate for the situation. An overly cocky attitude, too much athletic or academic elitism, or sky-high athletic or academic snobbery are *not* appropriate behavior and can result in rejection.

5. Lack of research: It's painfully obvious when potential recruits haven't learned about the team, the college or the coaching staff prior to the interview. Use the Internet to research them all, and talk with friends, your coach, your athletic director, your counselor, and other recruits about them before each meeting.

Need it be said again? Prepare, prepare, prepare.

6. Not having any questions to ask: Asking questions shows your interest in the college and the team. Not preparing a list of intelligent, relevant questions is begging for disaster. C'mon, it's easy; suggested questions are listed in Chapter 4 – pick a dozen.

7. Not readily knowing the answers to the interviewers' questions: Anticipate and rehearse answers to the potential questions listed in Chapter 3. Practicing with your parents, your coach, your counselor, or a friend before the interview will help you to frame intelligent answers.

8. Relying too much on your "resume": Coaches recruit strong student-athletes, not a list of statistics and awards. Although a written resume can list qualifications and skills and open the door to a meeting, it's the interview that will portray you as a committed, responsive team player. Do you think the coach would rather recruit the worst player from the best team in the state or the best player from the worst team in the state? No, you don't know and neither does the coach … until after he or she meets them. Be who you are and let the chips fall where they may – find that *right-fit* school for you.

9. Too much humility: See "poor attitude," number 3 above – this is just the opposite. Being conditioned not to brag, players are sometimes reluctant to describe their accomplishments. Now is not the time to be too shy. Explaining how you reach difficult or impressive goals helps coaches understand what you can do for them. Be honest and forthright.

10. Not relating your skills to the coach's needs: A list of sterling athletic accomplishments means little if you can't relate them to a team's needs. Remember to convince the coach that you're the right player for his or her team because you can provide solutions to their problems and meet their needs.

And last, but certainly not least –

11. Tire kicking: Some recruits, particularly those who appear to be (or actually might be) "highly recruited," will essentially admit they're just "shopping" for the highest bidder (athletic scholarship-wise) instead of looking for the *right-fit* opportunity. This often wastes a coach's time and leaves a negative impression with coaches who you may easily run into in the future (see Chapter 10). Future encounters happen more often than you would believe, and for reasons beyond your (and often the coach's) wildest imagination.

These are the top 11 reasons recruits may not be chosen by a particular school. Remember, though, you are looking for that *right-fit* college for *you*, so if one door closes, look forward to opening others.

10 A MAXIM TO REMEMBER

Treat every coach at every college with the respect and honor you would give to your favorite coach.

Treat them as if they will be your coach *tomorrow*, because sometime in the future

... they just might be.

APPENDICES

The following three worksheets can help you to assemble the knowledge you'll need to properly prepare for your meeting with a coach. They can also help you in your personal decision-making process to balance the actual facts about a particular situation with the emotional side of that same situation.

Max-StARS **Know Yourself Worksheet**

Name	
College	

	Strengths (& Selling Points)	Weaknesses
Academic		
Athletic		

	Short Term	Long Term
Academic Goals		
Athletic Goals		
Life Goals		

	Positives	Negatives
This University		
Playing at this University		

Max-StARS College Evaluation Worksheet

Name	
College	

School Information:	Answer	Does it fit my criteria?
Location (City, ST):		☐ Yes ☐ Don't Care ☐ No
Size of town (Pop.):		☐ Yes ☐ Don't Care ☐ No
Drive (hours from home):		☐ Yes ☐ Don't Care ☐ No
Undergrad Population:		☐ Yes ☐ Don't Care ☐ No
Academic Ranking:		☐ Yes ☐ Don't Care ☐ No
Majors (I might like):		☐ Yes ☐ Don't Care ☐ No
Public v. Private	☐ Public ☐ Private	☐ Yes ☐ Don't Care ☐ No
Religious Affiliation:		☐ Yes ☐ Don't Care ☐ No
NCAA Division:	☐ DI ☐ DII ☐ DIII	☐ Yes ☐ Don't Care ☐ No
Team Ranking (RPI):		☐ Yes ☐ Don't Care ☐ No
Athletic Conference:		☐ Yes ☐ Don't Care ☐ No

Team Information:

Class Ratios:	__ Fr __ So __ Jr __ Sr	☐ Yes ☐ Don't Care ☐ No
Win-Loss Last Year:		☐ Yes ☐ Don't Care ☐ No
Amount of Team Travel		☐ Yes ☐ Don't Care ☐ No
Major Opponents:		☐ Yes ☐ Don't Care ☐ No
Leading Players:		☐ Yes ☐ Don't Care ☐ No
Captains:		☐ Yes ☐ Don't Care ☐ No
Most Players are from what Region:		☐ Yes ☐ Don't Care ☐ No

Head Coach Information:

Graduated From:		☐ Yes ☐ Don't Care ☐ No
Coached At:		☐ Yes ☐ Don't Care ☐ No
Win-Loss All-Time:		☐ Yes ☐ Don't Care ☐ No

Asst (or Position) Coach:

Graduated From:		☐ Yes ☐ Don't Care ☐ No
Coached At:		☐ Yes ☐ Don't Care ☐ No
Win-Loss All-Time:		☐ Yes ☐ Don't Care ☐ No

Max-StARS Interview Checklist

Name:	Interview Date:
College:	Interview Time:

Preparation	Com-pleted
● Complete Know Yourself Worksheet	☐
● Complete College Evaluation Worksheet	☐
● Research College	☐
● Research Team	☐
● Research Coach	☐
● Research Financial Aid	☐
● Finalize Student-Athlete Resume	☐
● Finalize time & location of interview with coach	☐
● Schedule an Admissions tour/visit while on campus	☐
Bring to Interview	
● Student-Athlete Resume (2 or 3 copies)	☐
● My Statistics	☐
● SAT and ACT Scores	☐
● High School Transcripts	☐
● Notebook and Pen	☐
● Directions to Location (Google-Maps, MapQuest, or GPS)	☐
Questions	
● Prepare to Answer Background Questions	☐
● Prepare to Answer Personality Questions	☐
● Prepare to Answer Motivation & Drive Questions	☐
● Prepare to Ask Team Questions	☐
● Prepare to Ask Program Questions	☐
● Prepare to Ask Coach Questions	☐
● Prepare to Ask Academics Questions	☐
● Prepare to Ask Campus Life Questions	☐
● Prepare to Ask Financial Aid Questions	☐
● Prepare to Ask About Your Status as a Recruit	☐
● My questions are written in my notebook	☐
Appearance	
● Dressed as if I am travelling with the team	☐
● Cell phone OFF	☐
Control	
● My parents know their role	☐
Post Interview	
● Debrief with parents and other advisors	☐
● Send follow-up emails to all interviewers	☐

ABOUT THE AUTHOR

Jim Plappert is acutely aware of the needs and concerns of the up-and-coming student-athlete. As the founder of **Max-StARS**, a college selection consulting firm (maxstars4u.com), he works with student-athletes every day. He has seen firsthand how overwhelming the process can be to those who are completely new to it and the missteps taken by those who did not have the guidance and the tools to balance the emotional side of the decision with the facts of the situation.

Jim has written a companion book, *So, You Want to be a College Athlete*, which details how to work through the college selection process itself. It provides the guidance and tools for developing a game plan to assist student-athletes in choosing that ***right-fit*** university – one where they'll thrive athletically, academically, and socially.

A former student-athlete himself, Jim has stayed actively involved over the last thirty years with his four children, starting in community recreational sports with coaching and then in various booster clubs. Jim is also involved with regional and national tournament management as the Tournament Director for EventHockey.

Jim received his secondary schooling at the Mercersburg Academy, has a BS in Mechanical Engineering from Carnegie-Mellon University, and earned an MBA from the University of Pittsburgh. He spent twenty years in industrial sales and marketing. Following that, Jim founded an executive recruiting and consulting firm and spent another twenty years helping people maximize their potential as candidates for the business world and helping his client companies find the best possible employees to meet their ongoing needs.

As a recruiter, Jim developed excellent networking skills and used that talent to meet with and talk to the "brightest and the best" coaches, players, and parents with regard to the college student-athlete selection process and, ultimately, how to best counsel the student-athlete to succeed in those efforts.

OTHER BOOKS BY THE AUTHOR

This book is a companion to the author's other publication in the area of college selection and recruiting for aspiring student-athletes and their families, *So, You Want to be a College Athlete*. Designed to walk the student-athlete and his or her parents through the earlier stages of the selection and recruiting process (as opposed to Interviewing with College Coaches which deals with one of the final steps of the process) this sister publication will help parents and high school student-athletes to initiate, clarify, and continue important, life-directing family conversations about college selection and recruiting – and of ultimately finding their *right-fit* school. It is due to be published in the summer of 2012. The Table of Contents for *So, You Want to be a College Athlete* follows:

So, You Want to be a College Athlete

1. Challenges
2. Participating in Collegiate Athletics
3. Tell Me About the NCAA
    a. Recruiting Terms
    b. Divisions
    c. Recruiting Process & Rules
    d. Eligibility Standards & Amateurism
    e. Clearing House (Eligibility Center)
    f. Events, Timelines, & Timetables
    g. Shirting
    h. Sponsored Sports
4. College Entrance Examinations: SAT's and ACT's
5. Academic Index
6. Title IX
7. Finances & Scholarships
8. Committing (National Letter of Intent and "Likely Letters")
9. College Selection: Do Your Research
    a. Know Yourself
    b. Know the School
    c. Know the Coach
    d. College Visits
10. Student-Athlete Resumes: What Works
11. Contacting College Coaches
    a. Email Addresses
    b. Social Networking Accounts
12. Showcases, Combines, Camps, Clinics
13. Videos
14. Club & Intramural Sports
15. Sleep For Athletic Success
16. Sports Psychology
17. Parent's Advice and Support
18. What now?
19. Closing the Deal
20. Breaking Up is Hard To Do

ACKNOWLEDGEMENTS

This book represents the distillation of over two decades of knowledge garnered while working in the executive recruiting industry coupled with years of coaching at the recreational and club level, running regional and national athletic tournaments and showcases, countless years of booster club activities, and recent experiences learned while assisting young high school athletes in their quest to "take it to the next level" and compete in the collegiate arena. The interviewing skills and techniques offered herein were part and parcel to my daily activities during my nearly two decades of association with some of the brightest and most talented executive recruiters I ever had the joy of working with both during my sojourn as a franchise owner at Management Recruiters International and in running my own private firm, Newtown Consulting Group.

It is difficult, after all of those years, to exactly remember what was the groundbreaking work of others or twists on the process that I developed by myself. With that in mind, I would specifically like to credit contributions from the staff and fellow franchise owners at MRI.

Additionally, I would like to thank the countless coaches, players, and parents who I worked with or simply chatted with over the years for their contributions to my ever-growing knowledge of the athletic recruiting process. Lastly, a special "shout-out" to the college coaches, club directors, athletic directors, parents, and student-athletes who helped me with the difficult editing and publishing phases of this book – my eternal gratitude!

JFP
June, 2012

Max-StARS

★ **NCAA Rules & Process Consulting**
★ **College Guidance and Selection Assistance**
★ **Student-Athlete Resume Preparation**
★ **Marketing & Visibility Campaigns**
★ **Interview Preparation, Guidance & Practice**

Need help? Contact the author at **Max-StARS:**

Email Jim Plappert at: info@maxstars4u.com
Visit: www.maxstars4u.com

Made in the USA
Charleston, SC
18 December 2012